Can You Find It?

Sports
A Can-You-Find-It Book

by Lauren Kukla and
Aruna Rangarajan

PEBBLE
a capstone imprint

Bunches of Balls

Can you find these things?

goldfish

lacrosse stick

baseball glove

cherries

fish bones

barbell

sneaker

hamster

diamond

watermelon

Play Ball

Can you find
these things?

whale

cap

donut

strawberry

bow

cardinal

golden egg

gingerbread man

cat

French bread

In the Locker Room

Can you find these things?

flag

lock

face mask

frog

 ladybug

 toothpaste

 candy

 ghost

 watering can

tropical fish

GOOAAAL!

Can you find these things?

 jar

 dinosaur

 hot dog

 broccoli

dumbbell

gorilla

cactus

bowling pin

snowman

lollipop

Outdoor Fun

Can you find
these things?

dolphin

octopus

buoy

sand
dollar

paw print

lizard

ice-cream cone

mushroom

shovel

dove

Touchdown!

Can you find
these things?

owl

lemon

rat

bird

hat

rocket
ship

pretzel

acorn

rabbit

mustache

Trophy Time

Can you find these things?

 bananas   dragonfly   cheese   jack-o'-lantern

ambulance

notebook

star

stocking

shoe

peppers

Rockin' Rackets

Can you find these things?

tape measure

dog bone

waffle

ballet slippers

 scissors

 alien

 heart

 rose

 carrot

 croissant

Dream Team

Can you find
these things?

zebra

tooth

boom box

penny

eggplant

headphones

bulb

hat

sea star

bike

Wild Wheels

Can you find these things?

crown

baby carriage

seashell

figure skate

 tiger

 candle

 star

 camera

 bear

 sea lion

Basketball Fun

Can you find these things?

T-shirt

cloud

koala

sunglasses

 elephant pineapple avocado baby bottle corn domino

Celebrate Sports

Can you find these things?

saxophone

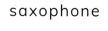

lightning bolt

horseshoe

bathing suit

 keyboard

 sea turtle

 pastry

 sandal

 pencil

 boat

On the Ice

Can you find
these things?

rooster

pig

trophy

spotted
dog

pin

swan

ladybug

cowboy
boot

horse

clothespin

jellyfish

mitten

bottle

cow

dice

coffee cup

butterfly

puzzle piece

rainbow

truck

Psst! Did you know that a pair of blue swim shorts was hiding in EVERY PUZZLE in this book?

It's true! Go back and look!

Look for other books in this series:

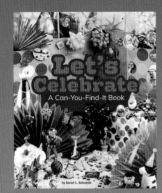   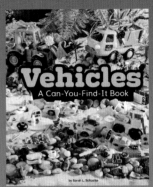

Pebble Sprout is published by Pebble, an imprint of Capstone.
1710 Roe Crest Drive, North Mankato, Minnesota 56003
capstonepub.com

Library of Congress Cataloging-in-Publication Data is available on the Library of Congress website

ISBN: 9781666397093 (hardcover)
ISBN: 9780756572747 (paperback)
ISBN: 9780756572488 (ebook PDF)

Image Credits: Scenes by Mighty Media/Lauren Kukla, Aruna Rangarajan
Shutterstock: Alex Kravtsov, cover (stadium), Gino Santa Maria, cover (baseball bats)

Printed and bound in China. PO5130